DEBATING DEFINITIONS

Eve Baker

Published by New Generation Publishing in 2022

Copyright © Eve Baker 2022

First Edition

The author asserts the moral right under the Copyright, Designs and Patents Act 1988 to be identified as the author of this work.

All Rights reserved. No part of this publication may be reproduced, stored in a retrieval system or transmitted, in any form or by any means without the prior consent of the author, nor be otherwise circulated in any form of binding or cover other than that which it is published and without a similar condition being imposed on the subsequent purchaser.

ISBN

    Paperback   978-1-80369-276-0
    Ebook   978-1-80369-277-7

www.newgeneration-publishing.com

New Generation Publishing

The Greater London Youth Foundation, a registered charity, endeavours to help young people to advance in life through the provision of recreational and leisure time activities. These activities are designed to improve and develop skills, self-esteem, confidence, and capabilities to enable them to participate in society as mature and responsible individuals.

A special thanks to all the members of Brent Youth Debates and Debating on Zoom, who motivated me to write this book.

It is better to debate a question without settling it than to settle a question without debating it—Joseph Joubert

FOREWORD

We have been running debating sessions face to face and online for many years. Over this time, various ideas and concepts have come up. Sometimes debates are hindered because the participants have limited knowledge of a range of philosophical thoughts, and time does not allow for in-depth explanations. We could forever remain at the beginner's level because our participants are unfamiliar with the plethora of 'ideas' out there, other than their own points of view. We don't expect everyone to know everything about everything; after all, knowledge is a work in progress.

This book offers a brief overview of the ideas raised during our debating sessions. You don't have to be a member of our group to read this book. We urge you to write brief paragraphs about your favourite philosophy, philosopher, concept, or idea in a journal. When you have lots of definitions in your intellectual toolbox, you might never lose an argument again.

CONTENTS

FOREWORD i
DEFINITIONS 1
DEBATING MOTIONS 106
A FINAL NOTE 121

DEFINITIONS

It would be impossible to define each concept in detail. After all, philosophers have written great tomes of work; others have criticised their ideas and proposed new ideas. We have tried not to offer any opinions as to whether theories are good or bad or better. Ideas, concepts, and situations have been developed within periods and context.

The only order that we use in compiling these definitions is that of the alphabet. The only reason for including them here is that the topic areas have come up in debates in some form or another.

A

Absurdism

Absurdism is the belief that humans live in a chaotic world that has no purpose. If the universe makes no sense and has no meaning, we are left to create meaning for ourselves. The myth of Sisyphus is an analogy of the absurdity of life. Sisyphus was a mythological Greek figure who was the founder of the ancient Greek city of Corinth. The Greek gods punished Sisyphus for tricking his way out of the underworld by forcing him to roll a massive boulder up a hill, only to watch it roll down again. Rolling the boulder up a slope every day for eternity was punishment for Sisyphus because the task was meaningless. Like life, some things can be pointless, yet we have no choice but to carry on and suffer.

Aesthetics

Aesthetics is the branch of philosophy that deals with the nature of beauty and the way we express beauty. It examines preferences, judgements, and tastes towards art and other objects of appreciation.

Aesthetics consider these questions: why do we find things beautiful? What makes something a piece of art?

Agnosticism
Agnostics believe that humans can never know whether God does or does not exist because God exists outside of the material world. As such, agnostics do not deny the possibility that God might exist but believe that it is impossible to prove or disprove God's existence.

Algorithms
Algorithms are a system of rules to determine the order of things based on coded criteria. The results from algorithms are analysed, from which we make decisions or solve problems.

Organisations use algorithms to find out what we buy, who we love, which leaders we vote for, etc.

Ally
An ally advocates for and supports community members other than their own and reaches across differences to achieve mutual goals. An ally is a person who may not share the sexual orientation or gender identity of a lesbian, gay,

bisexual and transgender person but who supports sexual and gender diversity and challenges homophobic, transphobic and heterosexist remarks, behaviours, institutions, and systems. This term also applies to champions of other political issues like the Black Lives Matter and MeToo movements.

Anarchism
Anarchism comes from ancient Greek and means *without a ruler* and the absence of government. The freedom of individuals without hierarchical interference is the ideal society. Individualist William Godwin (1756 – 1836) thought governments corrupt society because people become dependent and ignorant. He believed that individual rights were more important than the state.

Androgyny
Androgyny is a gender expression that has elements of both masculinity and femininity.

Antisemitism
Antisemitism is hostility against Jewish people. Antisemitism shows up in many ways, ranging from words of hatred or discrimination against individual Jews to organised pogroms. Entire Jewish communities have experienced

attacks, and there have been expulsions, persecutions, and massacres throughout history.

A priori

A priori is a thing that is a known fact before any worldly experience. In other words, information that does not come from learned behaviour.

Kant (1724 – 1804) stated that this was knowledge independent of all experiences.

A posteriori

A posteriori is a thing that is known to be true or false only through worldly experience. In other words, the knowledge that comes from learned experience.

Asexual

Someone who is asexual does not experience sexual attraction towards other people. However, asexual people can still have romantic, emotional, affectional, or relational attractions to other people.

Assigned Gender

People are assigned a gender at birth, based on visible genitalia.

Atheism
Atheism is disbelief in the existence of one God or multiple gods.

Autocracy
Autocracy is a system of government in which absolute power is held by one person, without any legal or political restraints on their actions. Absolute monarchies exist in Saudi Arabia, the United Arab Emirates, Oman, Brunei and Eswatini.

B

Behaviourism
Behaviourism is a branch of psychology that focuses exclusively on observable phenomena, such as emotions, memories, and motives. B.P Skinner, Ivan Pavlov and John B. Watson are considered the pioneers of modern behaviourism.

In an experiment on a young boy named Albert, Watson made a loud noise whenever a rat came near the child. Albert was not afraid of the rat at first but became terrified. Watson was even able to make Albert afraid of a teddy bear. Watson called this 'conditioning'. He advised parents against showing affection to their children, as this would spoil them. Watson was not interested in the mind and thoughts. He thought that how people behaved was the most important thing. Watson suggested that your environment determines your intelligence, temperament, and personality.

Watson thought he could shape a person to behave in different ways. He believed he could condition children to become doctors, lawyers, artists, even beggars when they grew up.

Black Lives Matter
#BlackLivesMatter started in 2013 in the USA in response to the acquittal of Trayvon Martin's accused murderer. The Black Lives Matter Global Network Foundation is a worldwide organisation in the USA, UK, and Canada, whose mission is to eradicate white supremacy and build local power to intervene in violence inflicted on black people. The originators of the hashtag and call to action, Alicia Garza, Patrisse Cullors, and Opal Tometi, expanded their project into a national network of over thirty local divisions between 2014 and 2016. The overall Black Lives Matter movement consists of decentralised hubs of activists with no formal structure or leader. The campaign returned to national headlines and gained further international attention during the global protests in 2020 following the murder of George Floyd by Derek Chauvin, a police officer.

Malcolm X (1925–1965) believed violent resistance was legitimate and necessary to combat injustice; a sharp contrast to the views of Martin Luther King Jr. Malcolm X publicly criticised Martin Luther King for encouraging peaceful protest.

Martin Luther King Jr. (1929–1968) organised numerous demonstrations, including the March on Washington. Mahatma Gandhi's non-violence strategy inspired him. King encouraged his followers to control and channel their anger into civil disobedience instead of fighting.

Barack Obama (1961-) believes that we can change the world by being kind and respectful to each other and that we cannot change the problems of our time unless we work together. Obama believes that we all want a better future for ourselves, our children, and our grandchildren.

Brexit
The ethos of Brexit was to take back control from the European Union (EU). The UK joined the Union in 1973. The British Government said that the UK would develop a new trading future and make new agreements with countries outside the EU. Being part of the EU meant no trading restrictions. People could move around freely. The UK left the EU on the 31 January 2020.

C

Capitalism
Capitalism is an economic system in which private individuals, rather than the state, control a country's trade and industry. These private individuals are profit-motivated and therefore have an incentive to provide goods to consumers more efficiently than the state. In this sense, capitalism is a way of distributing resources with no government interference. In contrast to communism, capitalism allows citizens to own and trade private property.

Karl Marx (1818-1883) believed that capitalism exploited workers who earned a wage while the owner sold the goods the worker helped produce for a profit. Marx called the owners the bourgeoisie because they had all the power. He called the workers the proletariat. Marx wanted the proletariat to collectively control the means of production so that everyone was equal.

Change
Change can be inconvenient and stressful. It often brings misery. If humans try to change too much, too quickly, it could end badly. But

change is inevitable. Revolutions can bring about tremendous change. For example, we didn't think hunter-gatherers suffered from disease and malnutrition until agriculture became prominent. The Industrial Revolution saw over-crowding, poverty, long hours, exploitation, and ever-changing technology.

Citizenship
Citizenship is the legal status of an individual in a political institution such as a state.

Cognitive dissonance
Cognitive dissonance is when someone holds two conflicting beliefs, values, or attitudes, which causes mental unease or discombobulation.

Collectivism
Collectivism is a social theory that prioritises the collective interest above the rights of the individuals who may compromise it. Collectivism involves constraining certain individual freedoms that have harmful consequences for society at large. China is a prime example of a country that has adopted collectivist values. China had, until recently, a one child per family policy, implemented to prevent overpopulation. Many western societies consider the freedom to have as many children as you want a human right.

Communism
Communism is a political system where all property belongs to everybody, and the state controls everything. The government allocates money, food, and healthcare according to need. Cuba, China, and North Korea are communist countries. The aim is to limit worker exploitation and eliminate economic classes. Communism operates differently in different countries, and you may hear the terms Stalinism, Leninism, Trotskyism, and Maoism. They are all versions of Marxism.

Conjecture
A conjecture is coming up with an opinion or making a decision based on false or incomplete information.

Corruption
We refer here to the people in government who abuse their power instead of using it to help the society they serve.

Countries
A nation becomes a country because it has a defined territory, a stable population, a governing body, and the ability to develop relationships with other states. There are 195 countries in the world today. This total includes

193 countries that are member states of the United Nations and two countries, the Holy See and Palestine, who are not members but observer states. Other sources say that there are over 200 countries. So which is it? There is no universal agreement on the number of countries on the planet. It depends on who is doing the counting.

Covid-19
The main symptom of coronavirus (Covid-19) is a high temperature. You feel hot when you touch your chest or back. You will have a new, continuous cough, and you will notice that you cannot smell or taste anything, or things smell or taste differently to normal. New variants have emerged with different symptoms. The Omicron variant is like a regular cold and can cause nausea, muscle pains, diarrhoea, and skin rashes. Many millions of people around the world have died due to coronavirus.

Culture
Culture is the customs of a population and includes the food we eat, the arts, beliefs, and institutions. The UK is multi-cultural. Citizens can enjoy various cultural activities in their daily lives.

D

Debating
Formal debating and competitions have followed the British Parliamentary debate process with two sides—the proposing side (the government) and the opposition. A debate is a formal argument on a specific topic. It usually ends with a winning side. The floor (or audience) can vote for the winner, or the adjudicator (judge) decides.

There are rules and a structure to debating. There are two teams, but there could be more than two teams or just two opposing speakers. There are many styles, but the main conditions involve each person or group coming up with a point they want to defend. They must maintain relevance and give examples and evidence. The last speaker will conclude their team's argument. The opposing team will do as much as possible to counter everything the proposing team offers.

Abstain
An abstainer chooses not to vote for either side.

Argument
An argument is a statement or reason for or against a motion.

Barracking
Barracking is posing multiple points of information without allowing for interruptions from anyone.

Loaded Question
A loaded question gives a limited range of responses. For example, when asked, 'Was that the first party you attended during the lockdown, Mr Prime Minister?'. A 'yes' answer would mean that he had been to a party, and a 'no' response would imply that he had been to a party.

Moderator
The moderator is the person who makes sure the debaters follow the rules and everyone keeps to time.

Motion
The motion (proposal or topic) is a statement for discussion and resolution. Topics usually follow the format this house believes. For example, this house believes everyone should vote at sixteen.

Opposer
The opposer is the first speaker of the opposition and is responsible for criticising the motion.

Points of information
A point of information (POI) is when a member of the opposing team in a formal debate gets to interrupt the current speaker. The speaker can accept or decline the interruption.

Proposer
The first speaker of the proposition is responsible for defining the motion.

Protected time
No one can make a point of information during the first minute and last minute of a speech.

Rebuttal
Rebuttals claim or prove that evidence presented or an accusation is false. A rebuttal can be made within speeches or as points of information.

A way to frame a rebuttal is to:

Restate the assertion - *you said the government protects its citizens.*

Refute - *the government does not project its citizen.*

Support your argument with data, evidence, or facts - *because six million citizens are unemployed, and the Trussell Trust network stated that the need for food banks has increased by 81% (2021-2022).*

Conclude - *because of this information, it is hard to see how the government protects its citizens.*

Seconder
The seconder is someone who backs up the proposer or the opposer.

Democracy
Democracy is a system of government that allows citizens a say in how society should operate. Although democracy originated in ancient Athens, it continues across the world in various forms today. Modern democratic systems generally rely on elected officials who represent their local communities. Democratic processes are compatible with other political systems, including liberalism (liberal democracy) and socialism (social democracy).

Socrates said that democracy is only as good as the educational system that surrounds it. He did not think ordinary people should have a say in political matters. Socrates thought only those qualified to lead should do so, and people should only be allowed to vote for a leader if they have a sound education that will help them make a decent selection. Further, he said that letting uneducated people vote could lead them to select demagogues. A demagogue is a political leader who uses charisma, instead of rational arguments, to acquire the support of ordinary people by appealing to their desires and fears.

Deductive reasoning
Deductive reasoning, or deductive logic, as it is sometimes known, uses a set of statements or observations to come to a conclusion or make a decision.

Determinism
The belief that whatever happens must happen because everything is an inevitable and necessary outcome of other preceding causes. This chain of cause-and-effect can conflict with the idea of free will. If all events are a necessary consequence of preceding events, people cannot choose anything other than what is needed and inevitable. Scientifically, an entirely mechanistic way of thinking about things would be determinism. The ancient Greek belief in essentialism and the Christian idea of predetermination are forms of determinism.

Dictatorship
A dictatorship is a form of government where all the power lies with one person.

The Doha Agreement
The state of Afghanistan began in the eighteenth century with the Hotak and Durrani dynasties. The country became free of foreign dominance, following the Afghan war of independence, under King Amanullah and became the Kingdom of Afghanistan. In 1973, the then monarch, King Zahir, was overthrown and Afghanistan became a republic. A second coup occurred in 1978, and Afghanistan became a socialist state. There was a Soviet-Afghan war in the 1980's, and by 1996, most of Afghanistan was captured by the Taliban.

The United States invasion in 2001 removed the Taliban from power, although they still controlled a large part of the country. The USA and the Taliban signed the Doha Agreement to end the Afghanistan War on the 29th of February 2020. One aspect of the agreement was to prevent al-Qaeda from operating in areas controlled by the Taliban. In August of 2021, the Taliban returned to power with the taking back of Kabul, the capital.

Dystopia

Dystopia is a term used to describe an imaginary state or society defined by great suffering, injustice, fear, and an oppressive government. In contrast to utopias, dystopias tend to be bleak and dysfunctional. These themes are in literature and film, with writers like Franz Kafka popularising the genre. Despite some similarities, dystopian fiction is distinct from post-apocalyptic fiction, and an undesirable society is not necessarily dystopian.

E

Echo Chambers

Echo chambers are an environment where you only hear information and opinions that are the same as your own. The danger is that this prevents you from being exposed to other opinions and arguments, thus reinforcing your own views, and leaving you susceptible to fake news and misinformation.

Echo chambers exist online because computer algorithms find out what we like and what we think. Your thoughts and opinions, likes and dislikes are sent back to you via social media. Information can come from anywhere. If we hear the same thing repeatedly, we may be in an echo chamber.

Confirmation bias means we will seek out information that reinforces what we already think and believe. Echo chambers occur anywhere that information is exchanged, such as online and face to face. If you lived in a small medieval village, you would not have access to a library, the radio, books, TV. So, in that respect, it would be like an echo chamber because you would hear from the same people all the time. Are facts ignored whenever they go against a long-held point of view? We must think very hard and engage with other opinions. Who are the experts? Are they professionals in the appropriate field, or are they reality stars and celebrities?

It's important to check multiple news sources to confirm that you are getting the correct information.

Empiricists
John Locke (1632–1704) believed that humans have no innate ability. He maintained that our mind is a *tabula rasa* or blank sheet. Our understanding of the world is shaped entirely by the ideas presented to us as we grow and develop, and it is our five senses that help people create ideas and information.

Epicureanism
The sole purpose of humankind is to seek pleasure and reduce hardship and pain.

Epistemology
Epistemology is the theory of knowledge. It investigates phenomena involving methodology, validity and scope that distinguishes belief, facts, and opinion.

Essentialism
Essentialists believe that all people have a predetermined destiny from which they cannot escape; in other words, essence precedes existence (we are born with a particular purpose).

Ancient Greek philosophers believed that we are born with certain traits and characteristics that give our life a purpose. Some people are born to be soldiers, and others to be doctors.

Essence is a particular set of core properties necessary for a thing to be what it is. The essence of water is one part hydrogen and two parts oxygen. Without any of those ingredients, it would not be water.

Ethics (moral philosophy)
Ethics is the branch of philosophy that examines human values, and questions which moral principles shape our lives.

Ethics has a relationship between the rightness and wrongness of human rights, punishment, and medicine. It has much to do with what we regard as a good life. What is a good life? Who makes that judgement? Does it mean not drinking alcohol and smoking, going to church regularly, being brave and doing good deeds? Does a good life mean not killing or lying?

Existentialism
Existentialism was developed in the nineteenth and twentieth centuries, and held that all people have the free will to determine their path and meaning in the world.

The most well-known existentialists are Søren Kierkegaard, Friedrich Nietzsche, Martin Heidegger, and John-Paul Sartre. They all believed that existence precedes essence. We are born without a purpose, and that there is no such thing as destiny.

We can exercise free will, while remembering that freedom is not the same as being carefree. We are responsible for ourselves, and we must find meaning. When this becomes difficult, it is called an existential crisis. Even if we have fame and prosperity, we may still wonder what our purpose is, why we are here and how we can make a difference.

Existentialists believe we must create our destiny and values because God does not exist. However, not all existentialists believe God does not exist. They take what is considered a leap of faith, but it is for the individual to find meaning and make the right choices for themselves and others.

F

Fake News

Language and the structures that underpin it shape how we see the world.

Stories can unite people. Fiction is entertaining but can also be used to manipulate. Emotion, experience, and trust play a part. A person can choose to widen the range of things they look at and study for information to help to identify fake news.

The Witchcraft Act of 1735 made it a crime to claim that anyone had magical powers or was guilty of practising witchcraft. Before this date, more than 50,000 people, primarily women, were executed because of the fake news that witches existed. The Salem witch trials started from rumours, and today's social media can cause fake news to spread without evidence in a similar way, causing harm to others.

False dichotomy
A false dichotomy limits the available options. A case in point was the disagreements and misinformation around coronavirus pandemic debates.

Discussions about the pandemic revolved around health and lives, the economy and livelihoods, indefinite lockdown and unlimited reopening, masks, or no masks.

Fallacies
A fallacy is misleading reasoning.

Ad hominem fallacy (Latin for 'to the person') The ad hominem fallacy occurs when the person's personality or background is criticised rather than their argument.

Bandwagon fallacy
The bandwagon fallacy suggests that the majority's opinion is always correct. Most UK citizens voted to leave the European Union, but this alone does not mean it was the *right* decision. It is possible that people were not fully aware of what they were voting for or that the majority made the wrong decision.

The appeal to authority fallacy
Sometimes we rely on older or more senior people to give advice, but it does not mean they know anything.

The hasty generalisation fallacy
People may make hasty decisions without having all the facts.

The slothful induction fallacy
This fallacy is when it takes a long time to make a decision. Or people may disregard valuable information and put it down to coincidence.

The Texas sharpshooter fallacy
The Texas Sharpshooter fallacy depends on pretending that good outcomes are based on skill and expertise and not because no one looked at the failures.

The anecdotal evidence fallacy
This fallacy uses personal experience as a substitute for definitive proof. Anecdotal evidence could be a single occurrence.

The middle ground fallacy
Compromising is not always the best way forward. It may create a dynamic that is not feasible.

The burden of proof fallacy
Sometimes it is not possible to prove something is true or false. However, if that is the assertion, the responsibility to provide evidence lies with the person making the case.

The personal incredulity fallacy
Often an idea is dismissed because it is difficult to understand, but that is no reason to disregard a case.

The 'you also' fallacy
The 'you also' fallacy means that when a speaker criticises their opponent, the response is a counterattack rather than to give a valid counterargument. Discrediting or personally attacking your opponent and retaliation is not in the spirit of true debating.

The correlation/causation fallacy
Debaters must be careful not to assume that because two things have coincided, there is a relationship, or one thing caused the other.

Inductive leap
An inductive leap is when you conclude something without sufficient information or evidence.

Inductive reasoning
Inductive reasoning is extrapolating (generalising) an occurrence and then coming up with a conclusion.

Scientific methods aim to overcome the problem of induction. Repetitive occurrences do not ensure that the same thing will happen again. Francis Bacon (1561- 1626) suggested that we should look for adverse outcomes to disconfirm hypotheses rather than find ways of confirming them.

Occam's razor fallacy
We may choose an option because it is easier to verify or carry out, but we should always look for other reasons why a thing has happened. The simplest solution is not always the best one.

Fascism
Fascists believe that you can create a more robust, greater society by eliminating all its weaknesses. It is a form of far-right authoritarianism which took off in Italy, Germany, and Japan in the twentieth century. Fascism attempts to unify a country into a supreme single, pure, political entity.

In addition, the control of society and people by the state would ensue. This structure, called totalitarianism, demands that citizens adhere to the government's demands and expectations. The single-party elite, headed up by a dictator, would oppose any competing political party. Fascism strives to get what it needs through violence and killing people who do not fit in or who protest against it. Deportation and executions were the usual methods used in fascist societies. Fascists outlawed unionisation and, as well as murder, promoted eugenics, censorship, and propaganda to achieve their aims.

Adolf Hitler (1889-1945) became the leader of the Nazi Party in 1921. We think of Hitler as the embodiment of modern political evil because he ordered the murder of millions of people across Europe. The Nazis killed seven million Soviet civilians, six million Jews, 312,000 Serbian civilians, 250,000-500,000 Romani people and 250,000 disabled people. After losing the war in 1945, Hitler committed suicide to avoid being captured by the Soviet Red Army.

Fast fashion
Fast fashion is copying garments on the catwalk and getting them into the shops within

days. Clothes give us an identity. Clever marketing, social media influencers and branding promote endless purchases. Instead of having two seasons a year, spring/summer and autumn/winter, clothes manufacturers provide up to fifty-two seasons to maximise profits. On average, people buy over sixty items of clothing each year, wearing them less than three times before passing them on.

The USA make only 2% of their clothes. China, Bangladesh, Vietnam, and Cambodia produce garments for the US market.

In 2015, textile production created more greenhouse gases than all international flights and shipping combined.

Feminism
There is no one type of feminism. Feminists are those who speak out about any injustices towards women and support social equality for all genders. The first significant change for feminists was being allowed to vote and own property. Before that, women needed male guardians to transact business on their behalf. Women were told they should be quiet and pleasant. Anger was not ladylike. Reproductive freedom and campaigns to speak out against female genital mutilation are still high on the agenda even now.

Mary Wollstonecraft (1759-1797) advocated education for girls and opened a girls' boarding school in Newington Green, London. She thought women might seem inferior to men because it was not widespread for girls to go to school, and they had to ask their fathers or husbands for permission to do things. Wollstonecraft asserted that women should have the same rights as men.

Free will

Free will is the belief that events are not simply the product of cause and effect, in contrast to determinism, since we can act freely and independently to shape our own futures. Are people free to do what they want, or are we influenced by fate, politics, biology, class, or race? How relevant is free will or determinism to the ordinary person? We all have different needs and wants. Are we defeatist or aspirational? Defeatists think everything that happens to them is caused by external factors. This thinking can lead to under-achievement and self-deception. People with many aspirations feel they can do anything they want. However, if things do not work out, they can become bitter and outraged. We can learn to understand and accept what is outside of our control. We also have the freedom to control our attitude to events.

G

Gender
Gender is not the same in all cultures, with masculinity and femininity serving as mutual opposites. Other cultures, such as Native Americans, have three genders. The third gender has elements of masculinity and femininity and plays a sacred role in their culture.

Every culture ascribes meaning to gender, basing it on genitals in the first instance.

Structural-functional theory keeps society organised and functioning. That means organising society into roles that complement each other. Hunter-gatherer men went out to hunt, and the women looked after the home. Men were physically stronger and did not have the burden of childbearing. These roles became institutionalised, even when physical strength was no longer an issue. There is no need for big game hunting now. Women performed gathering, fishing and small game hunting, and this was much more appropriate for feeding families. Boys are generally taught competitiveness and given action toys. Girls tend to learn expressive qualities to prepare them for nurturing by being given dolls. Society puts people into moulds and teaches them that they must fit into them to be considered desirable.

Symbolic interaction theory is what a person does, rather than the role that is innate or imposed on them. We demonstrate gender by the clothes we wear and our hairstyles. Body language and gestures are also a way of demonstrating gender roles. Women cross their legs, while men spread their legs when sitting on the train, for instance.

Social conflict theory suggests that gender is a structural system that distributes power and privilege to some while disadvantaging others. Here, men have more control. In recent history, women were not allowed to vote or go on to higher education.

M.A.A.B./F.A.A.B./U.A.A.B.
Male-assigned at birth/female-assigned at birth/unassigned at birth.

Intersex is a term for someone born with biological sex characteristics that aren't traditionally associated with male or female bodies. It does not refer to sexual orientation or gender identity.

Geocentrism
Many years ago, people regarded the Earth to be at the centre of the universe. Later, heliocentric models of the sixteenth century concluded that Earth, and all the planets in our solar system revolve around the sun.

Global Warming
In the last one hundred years, the Earth's temperature has increased, which is the result of human activities. Factories, power plants, and motor vehicles have used fossil fuels, like oil and coal, all of which results in too much carbon dioxide being released into the atmosphere. These gases trap heat close to the Earth via a naturally occurring process called the greenhouse effect.

The sun radiates energy to Earth, which our planet and the atmosphere absorb. Excess energy is released back into space. The greenhouse gases trap some of this energy, and the reflected heat warms the planet. As a result, weather patterns are changing, and the Arctic Ocean ice is melting. Rising temperatures could mean the disappearance of coastal areas, severe drought in warm regions and some animals becoming extinct.

Just 100 companies are responsible for 71% of global greenhouse emissions.

Greta Thunberg, born in 2003, is a Swedish environmental activist who has been raising awareness about global warming and climate change.

Alok Sharma was the COP26 president-designate for Global Warming, held in Glasgow in 2021. COP means the Conference of Parties, and the 26 refers to the number of times the meetings have happened. The parties are the number of countries that signed the 1994 United Nations Framework Convention on Climate Change (UNFCCC). COP25, held in Madrid, Spain, took place in 2019.

Government
The role of government still perplexes people.

Plato thought that the duty of government was to make sure people could pursue a good and virtuous life. Plato did not believe that ordinary people were qualified to govern. Only trained and qualified philosophers could do so.

Aristotle tried to understand government a little better and decided it was either for the country's good or those in power. He believed that a good government consisted of royalty and aristocrats, while an evil or corrupt government included tyrants and oligarchs.
Thomas Hobbs said that there had to be government because if left to their own devices, everyone would be horrible to each other.

Individualist William Godwin thought governments corrupt society because people become dependent and ignorant. He believed that individual rights were more important than the state.

In larger communities, citizens have the right to elect someone to represent their interests and make decisions on their behalf. In the UK, we select local councillors and members of parliament once every four or five years.

Most political systems around the globe have the concept of authority, legitimacy, and accountability. However, theocracy is a system of government ruled by the clergy in the name of a god, and the state's legal system upholds religious law.

Greenwashing

Adam Smith (1723–1790) argued for the efficiency of specialisation, the value of consumer capitalism, and the need to give wealthy citizens honour and status. A crucial part of Smith's thesis is that unintended consequences of intended action would benefit society. If someone decides to set up and run a business, they must ultimately employ others who will get paid. This doctrine has come under criticism for failing to consider that many companies negatively affect individuals and society, especially when multinational corporations can have products made cheaply by exploiting workers in developing countries.

Some companies will label goods as green or eco-friendly to boost sales. There is often no proof to back up this assertion. When a company states that its ingredients are natural, does that mean 'good'? Arsenic, uranium, mercury, and formaldehyde are natural products but poisonous. Often there is a trade-off. Companies may make some concessions, but this is minuscule compared to their day-to-day business. Some foods labelled organic can still include non-organic ingredients. Every product in the supermarket has a carbon footprint, no matter how green they are. Companies sometimes use fossil fuels in the manufacturing or the delivery of a product regardless.

Similarly, sports washing is when a corporation that produces unhealthy food sponsors a football or cricket team, and biscuit companies sponsor the British Olympics and television programmes.

H

Happiness

The United Nations World Happiness Report (2019) found Finland and Norway to be the happiest countries in the world. Although these people have a good balance of life there, they are not especially rich. The things that make a nation happy include good health, long life expectancy, freedom to make life choices, social support, generosity, and an absence of corruption.

Over two thousand years ago, Aristotle said that happiness was a balance between excess and deficiency.

What creates happiness? Is it wealth? Is it fame? The Harvard Study of Adult Development studied individuals over a long period and recorded the findings. For seventy-five years, they tracked the lives of over 724 men. They have found so far that social connections are good for us. Loneliness kills—people who are connected to friends and family are healthier and live longer. Those who are alone live shorter lives, they develop poor health, and their brain functioning declines sooner than those who are not lonely. It is not just about being surrounded by people however, it is the quality of those relationships that matter.

The harm principle
John Stuart Mill (1806–1873) was a pioneering liberal thinker who proposed the *harm principle*, which held that all rational, autonomous citizens should have the right to act freely unless their actions caused excessive harm to themselves or others.

Hedonism
The most famous Greek hedonists were Democritus and Aristippus. Hedonism is the process of living your life to experience pleasure and avoid pain.

Hinduism
Hinduism is one of the oldest religions, with over a billion followers today.

There are seven core beliefs.

Hindus believe in one universal soul, Brahman. Brahman is the universe and what makes up the universe.

There is a belief in an immortal soul, known as Atman. When you die, your soul will transmigrate to a new body.

Good or bad karma is the result of how you live your life.

The goal in Hindu life is to get back to Brahman, through Moksha, a process of enlightenment, liberation, or emancipation from the cycle of death and rebirth.

The Vedas are sacred books of knowledge.

Hindus believe that time is cyclical with no beginning or end. There are four great eras or Yugas, and we are in the last one, Kali.

Finally, Dharma maintains balance in the universe and decent conduct. If every living thing followed their Dharma, everything would go well.

Holocaust
The Holocaust was the genocide of European Jews during the Second World War. Between 1941 and 1945, Nazi Germany killed six million Jews across Europe. The murders took place in concentration camps, such as Auschwitz.

Human rights (Universal Declaration of Human Rights, 1948)

1. All human beings are free and equal.

2. There should be no discrimination regardless of race, colour, sex, language, religion, or politics.

3. Everyone has a right to life.

4. There should be no slavery.

5. No one should suffer torture and inhuman treatment.

6. Everyone is a person before the law.

7. Everyone is equal before the law. Everyone is entitled to equal protection.

8. Everyone has the right to be treated fairly by a court.

9. No one can be locked up in prison for no reason.

10. Everyone should have a fair and public hearing in court by an independent and impartial tribunal.

11. Everyone is innocent until proved guilty.

12. Everyone has the right to be protected by the law against interference and attacks and have privacy.

13. Everyone has the right to freedom of movement and residence within the borders of each state. Everyone has the right to leave any country, including their own, and return to their country.

14. Everyone has the right to seek and to enjoy asylum from persecution. This right may not be invoked in the case of prosecutions genuinely arising from non-political crimes or acts contrary to the purposes and principles of the United Nations.

15. Everyone has the right to a nationality. No one shall be arbitrarily deprived of nationality, nor denied the right to change it.

16. Everyone has the right to marry and have a family.

17. Everyone has the right to own things.

18. Everyone should have freedom of thought and religion.

19. Everyone has the right of freedom of opinion and expression.

20. Everyone has the right to freedom of peaceful assembly and association.

21. Everyone has the right to take part in the government of their country, directly or through freely chosen representatives. Everyone has the right to equal access to public services in their country.

22. Everyone has the right to social security.

23. Everyone has the right to work and have decent conditions of employment.

24. Everyone has the right to rest and holidays.

25. Everyone has the right to a standard of living adequate for health and well-being,

including food, clothing, housing and medical care and necessary social services, and the right to security in the event of unemployment, sickness, disability, widowhood, old age, or other lack of livelihood in the circumstances beyond their control.

26. Everyone has a right to an education.

27. Copyright law protects artistic creations. Everyone has a right to culture and art.

28. All freedoms should prevail around the world.

29. Everyone is subject to the law.

30. No one can take away your human rights.

Hypothesis
A hypothesis is an idea. Scientific tests can determine validity through meticulous research and observations.

I

Inflation
Inflation is an economic process, whereby the general price of goods increases, and the purchasing power of consumers decreases. Inflation occurs for a variety of reasons. One of these is quantitative easing, where the government prints more money, causing goods to cost more as money is worth less than before.

Hyperinflation is when a country experiences a rapid increase in prices of over 50% each month. Hyperinflation reduces the value of savings, encouraging people to spend their money quickly because of rising prices. As a result, there is less money for new enterprises, foreign investments, and trading. Hyperinflation can lead to political instability. Hitler used hyperinflation in Germany to play on people's fears and convince them that extreme action was needed to restore economic stability.

Impeachment
Impeachment in the United States is when a legal team brings charges against the vice president or the president for misconduct they think has been committed.

Individualism

Individualism is a social theory that prioritises the rights of individuals above the collective interest. Most Western countries adopt an individualist approach. Citizens have the right to protest and share controversial opinions on social media platforms across Western Europe, regardless of how disruptive these comments might be to a government. However, these rights do have limits in liberal societies. People can be 'cancelled' for spreading hate on social media. Individuals can take legal action for slander or libel against them.

Patsy Stevenson stood up for women's rights at a vigil for Sarah Everard. A serving police officer kidnapped and murdered Sarah in March 2021. The courts found that the police handling the event did not respect freedom of expression and the right to assemble. They were abusive and heavy-handed towards the women in attendance who were protesting peacefully.

Insurrection
Insurrection is a violent uprising against an authority or government.

J

Jingoism
Jingoism is extreme and aggressive patriotism that results in aggressive foreign policy.

Journalism
Journalists interpret and summarise complicated information in a way that the public can understand, then share through different media sources, such as books, articles, documentaries, and podcasts. Reliable information is good for society. News is, or should be, diverse, relevant, engaging, truthful, responsible, and objective.

K

Kinship

Kinship refers to our siblings (brothers and sisters), our parents, their siblings, our cousins, and grandparents. This arrangement is called the Inuit kinship system, which emphasizes the nuclear family. Other complicated structures exist, such as the Hawaiian, Sudanese, Iroquois, Crow, Omaha, and the Dravidian kinship systems.

Kinship is ancestry, the legal bonds of marriage or adoption. These are the bonds that we call family—mother, father, children, aunts, uncles, cousins and so on.

A family is a group of people related by blood or marriage and are likely to share a home, finances, and feelings. Families are not formal organisations. Families are a social institution.

Fictive kin are friends who are part of the wider family.

Family of orientation is the family with whom you have grown up with and learned social skills from.

The family that you create when you are an adult is your family of procreation.

The immediate family is the nuclear family and typically consists of parents and children (biological or adopted).

There are also single-parent families, as well as families with two fathers or two mothers.

The extended family includes aunts, uncles, cousins, and grandparents.

Marriages are not always about falling in love. Sometimes they are about creating stronger bonds between families and providing economic security. Some cultures arrange marriages specifically for this reason.

Endogamy is a marriage of the same social standing.

Exogamy is a marriage of different social standing.

Monogamy is a marriage of two people only.

Polygamy is marrying more than one partner.

Bigamy is marrying someone while still married to another person in a country where polygamy is outlawed.

Patrilocality is living with the husband's family after marriage.

Matrilocality is living with the wife's family after marriage.

Neolocality is when a married couple lives apart from any of their in-laws.

Patrilineal (father) and matrilineal (mother) kinship is the tracing of ancestry through a parent.

Structural functionalists emphasise the role of a family in socialising children and regulating what is taboo and unacceptable, like incest.

Social conflict theory focuses on the way that families perpetuate societal inequalities.

Symbolic interactionist theory focuses on interactions in family life.

Social exchange theory believes that relationships are a form of exchange between people. If there isn't an equal partnership, marriages can end.

Kleptocracy
Kleptocracy means ruled by thieves. Corrupt politicians take bribes and kickbacks by doing special favours for friends and family, allowing them to win lucrative government contracts. These politicians may open offshore bank accounts to hide any additional income they receive.

The Kyoto Protocol
The Kyoto Protocol (1997 and 2005) extended the United Nations Framework Convention on Climate Change (1992), which commits state parties to reduce greenhouse gas emissions.

L

Laissez-faire
Laissez-faire is an approach that requires one to leave things to take their natural course without interfering. As an economic theory, it requires that governments do not interfere with the free market. This is based on the belief that citizens and the economy work more efficiently when left alone.

Language
There are about 7,117 languages spoken all over the world. The world loses one language a week. In one hundred years, half the world's languages will be gone. Most of what we know about the brain is from English speaking scholars. The most spoken languages in the world are English, Mandarin, Hindu, and Spanish. The key to versatility in language seems to be grammar. Some scholars believe that the rules of language are innate. Some languages have grammatical gender, and some even a neuter class.

Liberalism (classical)
Classical liberalism is a political ideology that was developed in Europe at the end of the seventeenth century. Classical liberals were committed to individualism, liberty, and equal

rights, believing that citizens should have the right to live their lives how they see fit, so long as they do not harm others. The government's role is to create an environment that allows people to live how they want to, while making laws that prevent citizens from causing excessive harm to themselves or others.

Liberalism (neo)
Neoliberalism is a form of liberalism that was developed in the 1930s and 1940s and was then revisited in Britain and America by politicians like Margaret Thatcher and Ronald Regan in the 1970s. Neoliberals believe individuals cannot be genuinely free in society unless laissez-faire economic principles are adopted, preventing the government from interfering in private business activity through state planning. The Chicago School, with Friedrich Hayek, was a significant contributor to the development of neoliberal politics.

Neoliberals want their property protected. They do not want to pay too much tax, and they do not want any interference in how they run their businesses. They believe these goals require a free economy with minimal government interference. The only thing a government should do is protect its citizens from harm.

The Lucifer Effect
The Lucifer Effect is a term coined by Phillip Zimbardo, who pioneered the Stanford Prisoner Experiment. It describes the point in time when an ordinary person decides to engage in an evil action. We all have in us the capacity to behave kindly or cruelly, be caring or indifferent, creative, or destructive. The same situation can make some of us do evil, while inspiring others to be heroic.

The psychology of heroism is to be a hero in waiting, but most people are guilty of inaction. To be a hero, you must learn to be a deviant because you must be strong enough to go against the majority. Heroes are ordinary people who end up doing extraordinary things – they act. For instance, Sergeant Joseph M. Darby was the whistle-blower in the Abu Ghraib torture and prisoner abuse scandal. He later received death threats and had to go into hiding. Wesley Autrey rescued a man who had fallen on the train tracks, risking his own life. These two men are examples of heroes in waiting.

M

Masculinity/Masculine
Masculinity (also called boyhood, manliness, or manhood) is a set of attributes, behaviours and roles generally associated with boys and men. It is a combination of socially defined and biological factors. Both men and women can exhibit masculine traits and behaviour. Femininity/feminine refers to a set of attributes, behaviours and roles generally associated with girls and women.

Metaphysics
Metaphysics is the branch of philosophy that deals with the first principles of things, including abstract concepts like mind, matter, and language. Metaphysics also examines questions relating to free will and determinism, the meaning of time and space, as well as the nature of mind and reality.

Metaphysics considers what is *self*? How do we understand the forces of nature?

Minimalism
Minimalists like to keep things simple. They would have only a few clothes and no clutter in their home.

Misogyny
Misogyny is the hatred or dislike of women and girls. Misogyny manifests in numerous ways, including sexual discrimination, belittling of women, violence, and sexual objectification. While philogyny is the love and admiration of women. Philandry is a fondness for men, and misandry is the hatred of men. A philanthropist is a person who seeks to promote the welfare of others, especially through the generous donation of money to good causes. A misanthrope dislikes people and avoids human society.

Money
We use coins and paper that have no value in their own right as money in exchange for goods and services. Everyone believes in money. You have to trust that you can exchange money in this way all the time, every time, anywhere in the world.

Monotheism
Monotheists believe in a single God, who is all-powerful, all-present and all-knowing.

Morality

Morality stands for a set of standards and shared values. Some behaviour seen as immoral in the past is acceptable today. For example, having a child out of wedlock, eating in the street, swearing on TV are no longer considered taboo. Different societies regard morality differently.

N

Nationality
Nationality refers to where an individual was born. You also inherit your nationality from your parents.

Nation-states
Borders are imaginary lines that divide one place from another. This line creates identity and differences from someone else who lives on the other side. Organisations like the United Nations have agreed on where borders should be. Humans need to belong to a group and be part of a family and community for self-preservation. There may also have been a need for a leader – someone who was the strongest, or most charismatic, or had the most resources. Before countries, there were empires, city-states, and tribal lands. Landscapes, like mountains and seas, provide natural borders. Now, every piece of the world is a country with its own governing body. Around the 1500s, monarchs wanted people to become loyal to them, or they wanted more power. Ivan the Terrible was the first Tzar of Russia. He made efforts to unify the territories under his control. Similarly, by the nineteenth century, all the western world territories became nation-states or countries. The Peace of Westphalia Treaty

(1648), after the Thirty Years' War, took all the social structures that existed and made them equal entities with rights.

The West divided the rest of the world into colonies. The lines were arbitrary straight lines and did not consider communities, tribes, feelings, or language.

The name Britain came from the Roman word Britannia. 'Engla Land' was so-called because of the Angles.

Great Britain, established in 1707, referred to the kingdoms of England, Wales, and Scotland as they shared the same monarch. When Ireland joined in 1801, the title became the United Kingdom of Great Britain and Ireland. Since 1922, only England, Northern Ireland, Wales, and Scotland have remained part of the UK. The rest of Ireland became a republic in 1949.

Nihilism
Nihilism is the belief that there is no objective meaning to our lives. Newton, Copernicus, and Darwin doubted the existence of a God, who had supposedly created heaven and earth.

There were different explanations about the creation of Earth, the Creator, and how the world worked.

The North Atlantic Treaty Organisation (NATO)
The North Atlantic Treaty Organisation, established on the 4th of April 1949, is a military alliance between 28 European countries, the USA and Canada. NATO agrees to the collective security for all these countries and provides a mutual defence if attacked by external forces. The NATO headquarters is in Brussels.

If an enemy state attacks a member state, NATO will invoke article 5.

The result could mean that all members will take the actions it feels needed. It could mean another world war.

O

Occidental
Occidental is a term that refers to countries in the West.

Oligarchy
An oligarchy is a power structure where a minority of wealthy individuals have control over the majority.

Ontology
Ontology is the branch of philosophy that deals with the nature of human beings.

OPEC
The Organization of the Petroleum Exporting Countries is a partnership of thirteen oil-producing countries. They have 81.5% of the world's oil reserves and produce 44% of global oil. OPEC aim to stabilise and protect the oil market.

Opportunity cost
If you choose to do one thing, like take a holiday, you won't afford that new car; therefore, the cost of the holiday is forgoing the opportunity to get that car. If the government

funds the police, they may have to take money out of education.

Oppression
Oppression is the systematic subjugation of a group of people by another group with access to social power. Beliefs and practices can reinforce the status quo.

Orientalism
Orientalism describes how the West (Europe and the USA) see the Eastern parts of the world. The West often defines the East, including Africa, as weird, inferior, and uncivilised, and Europe as the opposite – superior and civilised.

P

Pandemic
A pandemic is when a highly infectious disease spreads across the world, affecting lots of people. Seasonal influenza is not classified as a pandemic as it is concentrated in large regions of the globe rather than being spread worldwide. The most dangerous pandemic was the Plague, also called the Black Death, which killed 200 million people in the fourteenth century. The 1918 influenza pandemic killed 50 million.

Paradox
A paradox is a statement that is also a contradiction. For example, the sentence, I tell lies may be true or a lie.

Paternalism
Paternalism is when a state or an individual with authority restricts the freedom of citizens against their will. This restriction is defended on the grounds that it is in the citizen's best interest.

Politics
Politics probably started in Athens around the sixth century before the common era (BCE).

Male citizens were encouraged to attend group meetings to make decisions. This democracy enabled people like Socrates, Plato, and Aristotle to think about the structure of society.

The business of leadership, enforcing laws, collecting taxes, controlling the military, and administering power is the backbone of politics. Citizens have the responsibility to pay taxes, vote in elections, obey the law, do jury service when required, and respect the rights of other citizens.

Populism
Populism is appealing to the fears and desires of ordinary people to attain positions of power in society. Populism has been a feature in politics for thousands of years and continues today. The Brexit slogan 'take back control' and Trump's promise to 'build a wall' are often used as examples of populism. Populist leaders tend to disregard political institutions that allow free and open debate. Instead, they create a 'them and us' mentality by scapegoating foreigners, journalists, the unemployed and single mothers.

Power

Power is the ability to get others to do what you want them to do. In civic life, power means getting a community to make choices. In a democracy, power is in the hands of the people, and we give the government power via our vote. In a dictatorship, power comes from the threat of force without the consent of the people.

Learning how power works is one way of ensuring that you are in control. Where does the power come from, and how is it exercised? For example, your teacher has power. Arguably, so do your parents.

There are several options used to gain power. They include physical force and violence. The power of wealth can buy results, resources, and people.

The use of law and bureaucracy make people behave in different ways. Social norms are a type of power. People will do what they think is acceptable. A good idea can motivate many people to act. There is power in numbers.

Preferred Gender Pronoun (PGP)

A preferred gender pronoun, or PGP, is simply the pronoun or set of pronouns that an individual would like others to use when talking to or about them.

In English, the singular pronouns are I, you, she, her, he, him, and it. I, you, they, and it are gender-neutral, but she, her, he, and him are gendered.

Public speaking
Public speaking is the cornerstone of effective debating. Here are some points to consider.

Practice breathing. Taking deep breaths will help voice control and make you sound less squeaky and high pitched.

Acknowledge your nervousness; everyone gets anxious, but if you know what you want to talk about, that is one less worry.

Learn your opening lines. Introduce yourself and thank the host for inviting you. You will come over more confident to your audience.

Use a mind map rather than a list of notes, as it is best not to read your speech word for word.

Use hand gestures to emphasise your points. Move around (but not too much).

Speak loudly and clearly, so that the back of the room can hear you. Don't worry about pauses. It will appear as if you are thinking.

Practise your speech. Record yourself if you can. You will sound different to yourself, because you will hear your voice through the air, not the bones of your head!

Use visual aids to support your words, but do not read out slides word for word or make them too busy.

Speak a little more slowly to be mindful of people in your audience whose English is not their first language.

Do not fixate on a few people in the audience. Scan the room with your eyes to give the impression of giving eye contact to everyone.

Suppose you must use a microphone. Do a sound check beforehand if possible.

Be aware of the time you are given to speak and stick to it as much as possible.

Use language and humour appropriately. If you use simple language, you will reach a wider audience.

Learn by heart your closing lines. Repeat your main points to the audience and thank them for listening to you.

Observe famous speakers (politicians, comedians, talk show hosts, etc.) on TV or YouTube and analyse what works and what does not work to develop your style.

Q

QED
QED in Latin means *quod erat demonstrandum*, and in English, *what has been demonstrated*. This abbreviation comes at the end of mathematical proof and philosophical argument. It means that a problem is solved.

Quality of life
The following list contributes to a good quality of life.
Physical health
Education
Employment
Wealth
Religious beliefs
Clean air
Personal safety
Work-life balance
A safe environment
Recreation and leisure time
Social belonging and a good upbringing
Good mental health
Security

If any or all are missing, it can result in an inferior quality of well-being, and may lead to poor mental health.

Priorities change depending on age and sex, context, and location.

Queer
Queer is an umbrella term to refer to all lesbian, gay, bi-sexual, transgender, intersex, and questioning people. It is also a political statement, which advocates breaking binary thinking and seeing sexual orientation and gender identity as potentially fluid.

Quietism
Quietism is a Christian philosophical term that is an antidote to today's overbearing loudness in prayer and worship. Quietists like to sit and meditate quietly. Instead of outward chanting and praying loudly, they rely on internal thoughts and contemplation. The essence of quietism is to forget about the rat race and slow down. It is not the same as meditation and mindfulness, but there are similarities.

Political quietism is a passive withdrawal from society, by refusing to participate in politics or comment on political issues. Religious leaders often practise political quietism to prevent people from conflating their spiritual teachings with their political preferences.

R

Religion

Zoroaster (600 BCE) told us to keep an open mind and listen. We should have good thoughts, never say bad things and do good deeds because one good action is worth a thousand prayers.

Epicurus (341 - 270 BCE) argued that there was no afterlife because our soul is merely a collection of atoms and that the gods had no concern for humankind. For these reasons, we do not need to fear death or divine punishment and should live in the pursuit of pleasure. The pleasures he meant were alleviation of pain, which is only possible through exercising the greatest of all virtues – wisdom.

A theocracy is when the law upholds and encourages the moral values of a society because it is believed that these principles are best for individuals. Often religious principles are enshrined in the legal structure of theocratic countries.

John Locke (1632–1704) argued against the divine rights of the monarchy. God does not choose the king. Locke proposed a social contract, meaning that society should be a consensus between rulers and subjects. Locke is famous for affirming that all people should have the right to life, liberty, and property.

Immanuel Kant's (1724–1804) most well-known concept is the *categorical imperative*, which he claimed was a universal moral law that all people should follow. You should only act in a particular way if you are comfortable with everyone behaving the same way. Only lie or break promises if you would not mind living in a world where everyone lies and breaks promises.

Ethics has a relationship between the rightness and wrongness of human rights, punishment, and medicine.

Resilience
Resilience is the ability to recover quickly from hardship and adversity. Developing competence, confidence, connections, character, contribution, coping, and control can all improve resilience.

Rhetoric
Rhetoric is getting what you want by using words. It could be in the form of books, tweets,

news information, or just talking. Aristotle said that there are three types of persuasion. *Forensic or judicial rhetoric* establishes facts and judgements from the past. *Epideictic or demonstrative rhetoric* discusses the present situation, such as a speech about some achievement that has taken place. *Deliberative rhetoric (symbouleutikon)* focuses on the future and promoting change.

Politicians use rhetoric frequently to persuade people about what might happen in the future if they want to pass a law (like what we will gain by leaving the European Union). It is also termed the rhetoric of activism. The speaker presents the possibility of what might happen to the audience.

We can change hearts and minds by using ethos, logos or pathos.

Ethos
Ethos is about convincing people with expertise and relevant qualifications.

Logos
Logos is to analyse and reason, using facts, figures, and data.

Pathos

Pathos appeals to emotion. Pathos involves impassioned pleas and convincing stories.

S

Scepticism
Scepticism is the belief that it is impossible to know anything with certainty. Absolute knowledge is unattainable, and doubting is central to all human knowledge and experience.

Secularism
Secularism is the separation of religion from the state. It leaves religious people free to practise their religion without bothering others. Non-religious people can live without the government imposing rules upon them through the law, education, health, and employment. There is freedom of religion and from religion, and there are no penalties or privileges from practising or not practising a religious belief.

Sedition
Sedition means to incite, assist in, or engage in rebellion against the government. Often significant violence is involved.

Sex
Sex is either of the two main categories, male and female, into which humans and most other

living things are divided, based on their reproductive functions.

Sexism
The cultural, institutional, and individual beliefs and practices that privilege men, subordinate women, and denigrate values and practices associated with women.

Slavery
Slavery is the forced labour that relies upon brutality, whipping, rape, branding and dehumanisation. During the transatlantic slave trade between 1514 and 1866, Americans and Europeans enslaved eleven million African people.

The countries most active in the slave trade were Portugal (3,894,059), the UK (3,088,776), France (1,309,424), the Netherlands (596,862), Spain (568,654), USA (377,613) and Denmark (103,988).

Social democracy
Social democrats do not want to get rid of capitalism but to redistribute wealth through taxation and for the government to provide public services and welfare.

Socialism

Karl Marx argued that capitalism generates class conflict between the bourgeoisie and the proletariat. Marx did not make an ethical judgement about what system should be adopted. He thought that socialism was the natural outcome of the economic condition of scarcity and the most efficient way of securing the goods and resources needed for survival.

Socialism is a social theory requiring that citizens contribute to essential things like health services, education, social services, social security, and pensions. Everyone can use what they need when they need it.

Under communism, most property and economic resources are owned and controlled by the state, not individuals. Under socialism, all citizens share resources equally, allocated either by a democratically elected government or another source of authority.

Sovereignty

State sovereignty is a principle of international law stipulating that all nation-states should have absolute control over what occurs within their borders. Sovereignty means equality between nations. There is respect for borders and the promise of non-interference.

During the post-war period, many nation-states made commitments to each other, essentially to prevent another world war and breaches of international conventions, such as the Universal Declaration of Human Rights. Violation of human rights, genocide and ethnic cleansing are unacceptable and could mean intervention from other countries. For instance, the invasion of Kuwait in 1990 caused the international community to impose sanctions on Iraq.

Many EU countries choose to be part of a union for peace and stability. We are more interconnected than ever before due to the need to tackle pandemics, global warming, and war refugees. These international problems make global cooperation necessary, but this also conflicts with the principle of sovereignty.

Statues
In June 2020, protesters pulled down the statue of Edward Colston in Bristol. He was a seventeenth century slave trader. Removing

statues is an attempt to challenge systemic racism and the oppression of people of colour.

Around the world, anti-racist protesters want monuments with racist and colonial legacies removed. There are over 800 confederate statues in the USA alone. People see these monuments as representing white supremacy and systemic racism. There are statues of these famous people.

King Leopold of Belgium
He created the Democratic Republic of Congo, a private colony. It was a slave labour camp where ten million Congolese died.

Robert Milligan
This man had a plantation in Jamaica and had more than 500 enslaved people.

Winston Churchill
This former British prime minister failed to distribute wheat to starving people in India in 1943. There was enough food in India at this time, but it was exported to support the war effort.

Christopher Columbus

Christopher Columbus had a role in the killing, kidnapping and exploitation of indigenous people in the Americas.

Statistics
Statistics is the study of data, including ways to gather, review and analyse it. We use statistics to describe situations or to make predictions.

T

Taliban
The Taliban emerged in the early 1990s in northern Pakistan following the withdrawal of Soviet troops from Afghanistan. The name comes from Pashto, meaning student or seekers of knowledge.

Tautology
Tautologies are sayings that repeat a meaning in a sentence.

Your team must get more points than the other team to win the game
A four-sided square
First and foremost
A new beginning

Theism
Theism is the belief in the existence of a divine deity, usually referring to monotheism. Polytheism is the belief in many gods. Deism is the faith in one God who created the Earth and made the law. Pantheism is one God who is everything in the universe.

Totalitarianism
Totalitarianism is a system of government that is centralised and dictatorial. The state has total control in a totalitarian system and there is little room for democratic processes.

Trade Unions
Trade unions protect workers' rights and negotiate better conditions and wages.

Transgender
Transgender is a term for people whose gender identity is different from their assigned sex at birth. Gender identity is not the same as sexual orientation. Gender identity is who you are, and sexual orientation is who you love. Some transgender people undergo hormone therapy or sex reassignment surgery as part of their transition, while some do not.

The World Health Organisation will no longer classify transgender health issues as mental and behavioural disorders.

Transhumanism
Transhumanism, a philosophical theory, holds that people can use technology and science to improve the human condition by enhancing things like mood and length of life. Gene

editing, avatars, robotic implants, brain-computer interfacing are all examples of transhumanist innovations. The goal is to create faster, wiser, more fertile, and disease-resistant human beings.

U

Unconscious bias
Unconscious bias suggests that your actions come about through habit and reflexes. However, behaviour is observable, and therefore, if you pay attention, you will recognise activities that are harmful to others. If you are the chief executive officer of a company, the police, or anyone in authority, you must be mindful of any actions you take that will discriminate against others. People with unearned riches and the tangible benefits of that wealth should not assume that poor people don't work hard enough.

United Nations
The United Nations (UN) aims to maintain international peace and security and develop international friendships. There are 193 countries in the UN, representing nearly all the world's sovereign states. The headquarters is in New York.

Utopia
A utopia is an imaginary place or society that is perfect for its people. Humans live in harmony with nature, and there is no need for crime or anything to go wrong. A dystopia is the opposite. There, society is bleak and cruel.

V

Value theory

Value theory is the study of the concept of value and what it entails in relation to ideas, objects, people, or anything that is considered valuable or essential. Value theory is central to economics. Resources are scarce, and people have unlimited wants. Therefore, we need systems to distribute these resources. The distribution will largely depend on the way we decide to value different goods.

Capitalism holds that the forces of supply and demand determine the value of items; high demand and low supply make an item expensive, while low demand and high supply make an item cheap.

Communism holds that the cost of extracting the raw materials and processing these materials into goods determines the price. If extraction and manufacturing costs are high, the item will be expensive, and if they are low, it will be cheap.

Voting in the UK

The UK has 650 parliamentary constituencies. Each constituent has an MP in the House of Commons. You must be eighteen years of age and over to vote. There are about 46,000,000 registered voters who cast their votes on polling day. They can choose one person from a list of candidates. The candidates who get the most votes in their constituency win a seat in Parliament.

The Queen invites the political party that wins the most MPs to form the Government, lead the country and select a Prime Minister. A good majority is 326 seats. If there isn't an overall majority, we get a *hung parliament*. This forces parties to form alliances to secure enough votes to pass laws and make decisions. At the time of the elections, the party in power would be the first to form a government by a *coalition* arrangement with another political party.

Many countries use a proportional voting system. The party that wins half of the total votes get half the available seats in their parliaments. Not in the UK. The UK system is called 'first past the post.' This same system exists in Canada, India, parts of the Caribbean and many African states.

Voting in the USA

The Election Year occurs every four years in the USA. It starts with what is called the Primaries. The Democrats and Republicans select their candidate. Every registered voter can vote for either the Democrat or Republican party. In some states, you can only vote if you are a member of one of those parties.

Electoral College

Citizens do not vote directly for the president. They are voting for delegates, or the Electoral College, who will vote for the president. The Electoral College is a process, not a place. It is a collection of men and women elected by each state to vote for a US president. Electors vote for a president on the first Monday after the second Wednesday in December, during election time.

There are 538 electors (delegates) who make up their Electoral College.

Each US state gets the number of electors according to the size of the population. California has fifty-five delegates, Florida twenty-nine and Texas thirty-eight. Most states have less than ten.

Winner takes all
If a state has twenty electors, like Illinois, and the Democrats win 60% of the votes and the Republicans 40%, the electors coming out of that state will be Democrats. A candidate can win in thirty-nine out of fifty states and not become president because the other eleven have many more electors. The winner needs 270 votes to become president.

W

Women's rights
Women's rights are the rights and entitlements claimed for women and girls all over the world. In some countries, these rights concern law, local customs, and behaviour.

Rights for women include the right to live free from violence and discrimination; to enjoy the highest attainable standard of physical and mental health; to have an education; to own property; to vote, and to earn an equal wage.

Worldview
A worldview is a particular philosophy of life or conception of the world.

X

Xenophobia

Xenophobia is the fear and hatred of foreigners or those from a different culture. The Romans thought that those outside their walls were barbarians to be conquered and enslaved. Xenophobia often plays a role in populist leadership, by creating a foreign enemy who can be blamed for domestic problems.

Exers or Generation X

This is the generation following the *baby boomers* of the 1950s and come before the *millennials* of the 1990s and 2000s. The period for Generation X is approximately the late 1970s to the early 1980s. This was the time of MTV, the music video channel, punk, post-punk, and heavy metal.

Y

Young people
Childhood ends at the age of eighteen.

Adolescence is the phase of life between childhood and adulthood, from ages eleven to nineteen. It is a unique stage of human development and an important time for laying the foundations for good health. Adolescents experience rapid physical, cognitive and psychosocial growth. Adolescence is a time to find an identity and to work out who you want to become.

Young people have rights. They have the right to life, survival, development, education, and an adequate standard of living. There should be freedom from violence, abuse, and neglect. Young people ought to be able to express views on matters affecting them, including legal proceedings.

Young people suffer discrimination and cannot vote until they are eighteen in the UK. They earn less than adults doing the same job. Some young people suffer from another type of discrimination called adultification bias. Adultification bias, a form of racial prejudice, is when adults, especially those in authority, treat children, particularly black children, as if they were older and more mature than their actual age.

However, young people do have a right to some things. Gillick competency is usually about medical advice, but it can assess whether a child is mature enough to decide any treatment they want without parental consent or knowledge. Fraser guidelines refer to advice and treatment about contraception and sexual health when professionals work with under sixteen-year-olds. A young person can also make decisions about their living arrangements with the support of social workers.

Z

Zionism
Zionism is a movement that aims to develop and maintain a Jewish state in Israel, because of the historical and religious connection between Jewish people and this territory. Jews have faced persecution for thousands of years, and Zionism is a response to mistreatment and antisemitism.

Zoroastrianism
The prophet Zoroaster started Zoroastrianism 3500 years ago. Zoroastrianism was the dominant religion of Iran for over 1000 years. The priests were called Magi. The ancient Greeks thought that they had magic powers and that is where we get the words 'magic' and 'magician.' The three wise men who visited Jesus in his manger were Zoroastrian Magi. Some Iranian Zoroastrians fled to India due to Arab invasions and persecutions and formed the Parsi community.

Zoroastrians believe in one God, Ahura Mazda. He is benevolent and kind.

DEBATING MOTIONS

Exercises

Find arguments FOR and AGAINST each debate motion listed.

This house believes there is no value in having a monarchy in the twenty-first century.

This house believes statues glorify the past, and communities should have the right to remove them.

This house believes revolutions should be avoided because they almost always cause more harm than good.

This house believes technology will never allow us to create a perfect world.

This house believes we should embrace the fact that marriage is going out of fashion.

This house believes social media is an effective way of sharing information.

This house believes that journalists report on what is popular rather than what is important.

This house believes that people are slow to adapt change.

This **house believes** social media will make people lonelier in the long run.

This house believes culture develops organically and cannot be changed quickly.

This house believes religious values should inform public policy.

This house believes customs and traditions are more important than many civil rights.

This house believes young people should not be taught anything about sex until they are sixteen.

This house believes parents should be able to choose whether their children learn about LGBT+ issues in school.

This house believes we should work a four-day week.

This house believes it is unethical to tamper with human nature.

This house believes people cannot monitor their moral behaviour.

This house believes the world would be a better place if everyone always told the truth.

This house believes people are generally bad at behaving morally.

This house believes a degree of inequality is desirable in society.

This house believes it is important to always look smart.

This house believes Sisyphus could find happiness despite his punishment.

This house believes that it is hard for humans to be ethical.

This house believes that all governments are corrupt, and that is something we need to accept.

This house believes the government is mostly concerned with commerce.

This house believes that if the government gave better information, we would be able to make more informed decisions.

This house believes people are generally decent human beings.

This house believes to have a second language is to have a second soul.

This house believes that being happy is not a realistic goal.

This house believes that it is wrong to favour friends and family over others.

This house believes criminals are a creation of society.

This house believes we should all live a good life.

This house believes male gender traits are more valuable in society.

This house believes that you cannot create your destiny, as it depends upon your upbringing.

This house believes the language we speak shapes the way we think.

This house believes that young people are not capable of making mature decisions.

This house believes gender is a spectrum.

This house believes we will never live in a world without war.

This house believes people are not good at working together in groups.

This house believes humans are dangerous by nature and must be controlled.

This house believes humans are tribal beings who will always form gangs.

This house believes young people should be taught how to fight before they are taught how to read.

This house believes sticks and stones may break our bones, but words will never hurt us.

This house believes populism enabled Trump to be elected the 45th president of the USA.

This house believes xenophobia has contributed to the UK leaving the EU.

This house believes that in a globalized world, there is no reason for borders.

This house believes that we are not doing as much as we can to reduce global warming.

This house believes it is necessary to enact a world government to tackle global issues.

This house believes that powerful countries should be responsible for keeping global peace.

This house believes people should be allowed to travel to any country in the world without any restrictions.

This house believes all supermarkets should be forced to source all produce locally.

This house believes Bitcoin should be internationally recognised as a legitimate legal currency.

This house believes torture is acceptable when used for national security purposes.

This house believes nation-states should never intervene in the affairs of other nation-states.

This house believes the European Union does not treat its member-states equally.

This house believes torturing terrorists is acceptable if it is done on foreign territory.

This house believes using drones to execute foreign enemies is unethical.

This house believes migrants should be forced to learn the language of the country they live in.

This house believes the government should prohibit the sale of tobacco.

This house believes sixteen-year-olds should not be allowed to join the army.

This house believes the government should force all people to go to church on Sunday.

This house believes citizens should not be allowed to own private property.

This house believes governments should always apply laissez-faire economic principles.

This house believes there are too many laws in most occidental countries.

This house believes it should be illegal to waste electricity at home.

This house believes sixteen-year-olds should have the vote in all local elections.

This house believes governments should provide all citizens with free healthcare.

This house believes it is necessary to test medical products on animals.

This house believes there should be no welfare state.

This house believes the government should legalise drugs.

This house believes we should implement positive discrimination initiatives across all professions.

This house believes capital punishment should be introduced for those who commit murder.

This house believes euthanasia should be a legal option for people who are severely ill.

This house believes anything that contributes to climate change should be illegal.

This house believes football fans caught racially abusing players should be jailed for a minimum of five years.

This house believes that if a politician lies to parliament and the people, they should resign.

This house believes suffering is part of life.

This house believes wealth is an essential thing in life.

This house believes we would be happier with less.

This house believes resilience is accepting your vulnerabilities.

This house believes that religion is the opium of the people.

This house believes that social media friends and likes won't make us happy.

This house believes lives that lack meaning are meaningless.

This house believes you become who you are due to a genetic predisposition.

This house believes you become who you are due to your upbringing and beliefs.

This house believes wealthy people are more likely to live happy lives.

This house believes religion is valuable, even if it is not true.

This house believes there is no way of disproving the existence of God.

This house believes that taking down a statue erases history.

This house believes we can love our pets more than people.

This house believes life has an objective meaning.

This house believes if God existed, then He would not have let the Holocaust happen.

This house believes we should adopt a vegetarian lifestyle.

This house believes local authorities should restrict the number of fast-food shops available.

This house believes the government should ban cars.

This house believes children do not need to go to school if they prefer to work from home.

This house believes people should recycle or be fined.

This house believes every young person should spend a year after school volunteering.

This house believes we should bring back military service.

This house believes Mother Theresa was not saintly in her lifetime.

This house believes we do not need the monarchy.

This house believes no one should disrupt society by going on strike.

This house believes communities should have the right to remove statues they dislike.

This house believes women are not equal.

This house believes women are superior to men.

This house believes that gender roles are from a Eurocentric perspective.

This house believes that lack of trust divides a nation.

This house believes that if the government can collect data on us, we should have data on the government.

This house believes wearing seatbelts, banning smoking, and taking the Covid-19 vaccine are violations of freedom.

This house believes citizens should have the right to commit suicide.

This house believes it is selfish to have broken any of the Covid-19 restrictions.

This house believes citizens should have to take a test before being allowed to vote.

This house believes prisoners should be allowed to vote in certain elections.

This house believes people should only be allowed to eat meat that they have hunted.

This house believes violent protests are justified under certain circumstances.

This house believes Martin Luther King's approach to the civil rights movements was better than Malcolm X's.

This house believes owners who do not take care of their pets should be sent to prison.

This house believes women should be allowed to have an abortion at any stage of a pregnancy.

This house believes we should go to Spain for our holidays.

A FINAL NOTE

We hope you have enjoyed this book and you will complete the Debating Motions exercises with friends and family.

Structuring thoughts and ideas develop critical thinking. Considering the points of view of others promotes empathy and understanding.

The world is changing all the time. What we thought was a good idea previously might no longer be so. It is okay to change your mind when different, more compelling information becomes available.

It is always best to back up ideas with facts and data and be aware that so-called facts change with new information. For instance, we once believed the world was flat.

Milton Keynes UK
Ingram Content Group UK Ltd.
UKHW010631010224
437088UK00011B/198